You Can Dough It!

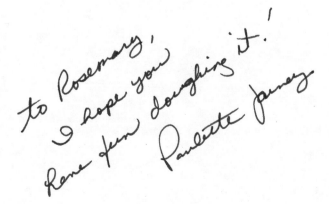

to Rosemary,
I hope you
have fun doughing it!
Paulette Jarvey

by Paulette S. Jarvey

ISBN 0-9605904-0-4

first printing December 1980
second printing April 1981
third printing November 1981
fourth printing October 1982
fifth printing March 1983

Hot Off the Press, publishing
7212 S. Seven Oaks
Canby, Oregon 97013

Contents

4

To very special friends who gave their encouragement, talent and, most precious of all, their time. For Suzy, Dave, Ruth, Joan, and my husband, Mike. Thank you.

edited by Suzy Jones
title, cover design, and line drawings by Dave Jones
page layout by Ruth Rodgers
paste-up, proof reading, and "About the Author" by Joan Humbert
black and white photographs by Mike Jarvey
cover photographed by Bill Werts Photography, Los Angeles, Calif.

Dough art is an especially satisfying craft. It can be enjoyed by everyone, although children under two years of age tend to eat it! People who "have no talent" or who are "all thumbs" can make mushrooms that look like mushrooms and teddy bears that look like teddy bears. You needn't be "artistic". Just follow the step-by-step instructions and photographs for beautiful results. It costs very little to get started. You will need flour, salt, a garlic press, aluminum foil, and, of course, this book. Then, you are ready to begin. You will be fine. In teaching dough art, I have had students full of insecurities begin class and end with positive feelings about themselves and their abilities. Relax and trust me. This is for fun. *You Can Dough It!* is the result of eight years of experience in creating, teaching, and selling dough art. One note, the designs in this book are for you to make for your personal use or gifts. All pieces are copyrighted and no one may legally sell these pieces without my written permission. I sincerely hope you enjoy doing dough.

Paulette Jarvey

DOUGH ART RECIPE

There are many but this is the best! Measure carefully.

4 cups flour
1 cup plain or iodized salt
1½ cups hot water (as it comes from the tap)

1. Pour the hot water and salt into a bowl and stir for 1 minute. The grains of salt will reduce in size but not dissolve.

2. Add the flour and stir until the water is absorbed.

3. Turn the dough onto a table or bread board and knead a few minutes. The dough is ready when it is smooth and pliable.

4. Keep the dough in a plastic bag so it will not dry out as you use it.

This recipe may be cut in half or increased by doubling or tripling the ingredients. It is best to use the dough within 24 hours. Left over dough should be stored without refrigeration in a plastic bag.

MIXING

TEXTURE OF DOUGH

- Too sticky: knead in more flour, however, the dough will remain soft.
- Too dry: moisten your fingers with water and continue to knead. If necessary, place the dough in a plastic bag and sprinkle with a few drops of water. Then set the dough aside for ½ hour.

TYPES OF FLOUR

- Bleached or unbleached flour works best.
- Do not use self-rising flour.
- Whole wheat and rye flours are not very satisfactory. They do not make as smooth and pliable a dough as white flour.

TO ADD COLOR

- For a bright color that does not fade, use liquid tempra paint.
- Put ¼ cup liquid tempra paint into a measuring cup and add hot water until the total liquid is 1⅔ cups. Notice that this is more liquid than the basic recipe requires. Mix as usual.
- Food coloring, dry mustard, paprika, liquid coffee or tea can also be added to the hot water. The total liquid should be 1½ cups.

SHAPING

JOINING TWO PIECES OF DOUGH

- Where dough touches dough it must be joined with water. Since water is used frequently, keep some nearby when working with dough.

THE USE OF ALUMINUM FOIL

- For each project you will be told when to place the dough onto a sheet of aluminum foil. When ready to bake, simply lift the foil and transfer it to the cookie sheet. The foil prevents the dough from sticking to the cookie sheet.
- Aluminum foil is also shaped into a form. Then dough is placed over the form to make larger, thicker projects. See page 39.

TOOLS

- Most tools needed for dough art can be found in the kitchen. The basic tools include: cookie sheet, aluminum foil, rolling pin, knife, straw, nutpick, and garlic press.
- For your convenience, each project has a list of tools "you will need."

GLAZING

The directions for each project will tell which glaze is to be applied to that project.

- Egg white, evaporated milk or mayonnaise is applied before baking. Each gives a shiny, light brown glaze.

- Egg yolk is painted on with a small paint brush. Apply it before baking for a dark brown glaze.

- For a vivid color mix food coloring in evaporated milk and paint before baking.

- Plastic cooking crystals can be used for a "stained glass" effect. Position them just before baking.

- Poppy seeds, sesame seeds, caraway seeds, mustard seeds all give an interesting textured glaze. Spread egg white on the dough before sprinkling on the seeds.

BAKING

WHEN TO BAKE

- Bake as soon as your project is made. If it is not possible to bake immediately, cover the dough with plastic until you can bake.

- Providing the oven temperature is as required for the dough, foods can be baked in the oven with dough art.

TEMPERATURE

- Bake at 325°. Most projects will take 1 to 4 hours to bake. Estimates for baking time follow each project in this book.

- Thin projects should be baked at 300° to prevent the dough from "puffing" up.

- Dough art over a form, i.e., bread baskets, jar lid covers, and napkin rings should be baked at 250°, and allowed to cool slowly.

TESTING FOR DONENESS

- When the dough is hard all over it is done. Test by pressing at the thickest part. If there is any give, continue baking.

- If baked too long, the dough will burn.

MICROWAVE

- Using a microwave is not recommended, because the dough turns white, instead of golden brown. However, if you do use one, please read on.

- Do not use aluminum foil or make any project with a foil form or a wire hook.

- Thin dough art projects can be baked in a microwave at a low temperature, if turned often.

AIR DRY

- Dough art cannot be successfully air dried. It cracks and crumbles too easily.

CHANGE IN SIZE AND SHAPE

- Usually there is no significant change in the size of a project. Occasionally, a thin piece of dough will lift up. If this happens, weigh the piece down with an oven proof pan. Next time lower the baking temperature 25°.

- If a project "puffs up" during baking, also weigh it down with an oven proof pan. Again, lower the baking temperature by 25°, next time.

FINISHING

PAGE 10

PAINT

- Use acrylic, watercolor, poster, tempra or model paints.
- Oil-based paints take too long to dry.

GLUE

- To attach dough to a board use a brand of craft glue that will dry clear and remain flexible.
- Silicone glue will also work but it is expensive.
- Allow the glue to dry 24 hours before hanging up the project.
- Flowers, ribbons, and rick rack can be attached effectively with most any type of glue.

SEAL

- All dough art must be sealed. A gloss acrylic spray works very well. Use several coats of spray to thoroughly seal the dough. If the dough project is glued onto a board, spray it after gluing. Always spray outside because of harmful fumes.
- Varathane, shellac, varnish, or even clear fingernail polish will also seal the dough.
- Christmas ornaments, projects handled frequently, and projects placed in a room with high moisture, must be thoroughly sealed. A polymer coating works very well.

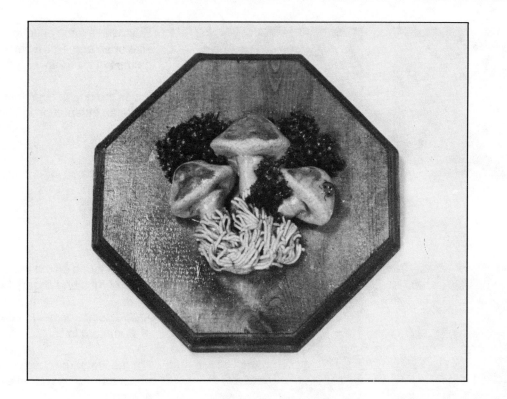

Mushrooms

Mushrooms are an excellent first project. They are a simple form and your success is guaranteed! Do not try to make "the perfect mushroom" — nearly any cap and stem will do nicely. After baking, mushrooms can be glued onto a stained wooden board, or into a shallow basket or picture frame. Small bunches of dried flowers, glued between the mushroom caps, add color. Instead of dough grass, real moss could be glued over the mushroom stems for another look.

YOU WILL NEED:

aluminum foil
cookie sheet
garlic press
knife
ruler
water
egg white

1 batch of dough will make
6 to 8 mushroom groupings

1

2

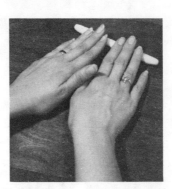

3

4

5

6

7

8

1   Start with a lump of dough about the size of an egg. Roll it between your palms until smooth.

2   Press the dough over your knuckle to make an indentation for the stem.

3   Put the dough on the table and with your thumbs and fingers form the cap.

At this point transfer the cap to a sheet of aluminum foil.

4   For the stem: roll out a coil of dough about as thick as your little finger. Cut a 4″ length.

5   Dip one end of the stem into water and insert it into the cap — water is necessary to bond the pieces together.

6   Make 2 more mushrooms. Place one on each side of the original. Dab water on the lower ends of the stems. For grass: squeeze dough through a garlic press. With dry fingers lift off the grass.

7   Lay the grass across the dampened stems. Repeat several times to cover the stem bases. For longer grass: squeeze dough once through the press — do not lift off the grass, but put more dough into the press and squeeze again.

*   OPTIONAL LADYBUG: Form a tiny ball of dough and join with water onto a mushroom cap. Paint after baking — see next page.

8   With your fingers or a brush, spread egg white on the caps (not on the ladybug). Bake at 325° until hard, about 2½ hours.

1

2

MUSHROOM CAP VARIATIONS

1 Form the basic cap, then pinch *little* ridges all over the surface.

2 Shape a ball between your palms. Place it on the table, and with your knuckle press an intentation for the stem.

13

3

4

3 Form the basic cap. With a straw press circles all over the top surface. Brush each circle with egg yolk.

4 Roll a fat coil about 2″ long. Place it on the table. With your knuckle press an indentation for the stem.

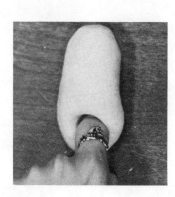

1

2

PAINTING THE LADYBUG

1 Brush the entire body with red acrylic paint.

2 For the head: with black acrylic paint make a dot at one end. For wing markings: paint 3 black dots on each side of the ladybug.

3

4

3 With a fine-tipped black felt pen, draw a line from the head to the other end of the ladybug.

4 Draw 3 legs on each side of the ladybug.

Flower Bouquet

This flower bouquet would be a lovely Mother's Day gift. It is one bouquet that will not wilt and die! Making 30 flower petals may not be very exciting, but the result is so pretty. If during baking your flower stems rise, weigh them down with an oven-proof dish. Then, next time lower the oven temperature by 25°. Once baked, this piece must be glued to a wooden board to protect the fragile stems. You may want to make different flowers. For a dogwood flower — make an indentation along the outside edge of each petal. For a variation in the flower center — make three small balls instead of one large ball. Or, for another look, paint colored evaporated milk on the center balls instead of the petals.

YOU WILL NEED:

aluminum foil
cookie sheet
garlic press
small paint brush
water
evaporated milk
food coloring

½ batch of dough will
make 5 flower bouquets

1

2

1   Take a small lump of dough the size of a grape. Roll it between your palms until smooth.

2   Flatten the ball between your thumb and finger.

3

4

3   Form a petal by pinching one side.

    At this point transfer the petal to a sheet of aluminum foil.

4   Make another petal. Dip the pinched end in water and place next to first petal. Pinched ends should touch.

5   Form 3 more petals. Join with water. Roll a small ball the size of a pea. Put a drop of water in the center of the flower and position the ball.

6   Make 2 more flowers. Be sure one petal of each flower overlaps a petal of another flower. Join with water. For the stems: press dough through a garlic press but do not lift off. Put more dough in the press and squeeze again. Do this until the stems are 4″ long. Lift off and position the stems as shown.

5

6

7   Make 3 more flowers. Place as shown.

8   For color: add food coloring to 2 T. evaporated milk. Paint each petal. Bake at 325° until hard, about 1 to 1½ hours.

7

8

Wired-Stem Flowers

These wired-stem flowers are very easy to make. Floral tape, which comes in many colors, is used to cover the wires. Brown floral tape, in particular, blends nicely with the natural color of the dough. For colorful flowers dye the dough with liquid tempra paint or food coloring. These flowers add a unique touch in dried flower arrangements. For a spring-time look, fill a clay flower pot with styrofoam and cover the top with moss. Arrange the dough flowers and fill in with some dried flowers, such as baby's breath. This arrangement will brighten any dark corner or windowless room.

YOU WILL NEED:

aluminum foil
cookie sheet
nut pick
straw
rolling pin
flower cookie cutter
knife
needle-nose pliers
16 or 18 gauge wire
brown florist tape

about 85-2" flowers can be made
from 1 batch of dough

1

2

3

4

7

8

1 Roll out a pancake of dough ¼″ thick. Press flower shaped cookie cutters into the dough.

2 Pull away the excess dough leaving the flower. With a straw cut out a circle in the center of each flower. (If the dough sticks in the straw, gently blow from the other end and it will pop out.)

17

3 Some flowers should have lines impressed on the top to form petals.

4 The blunt end of a nutpick makes a good design in the center.

At this point transfer all flowers to a sheet of aluminum foil.

Bake at 325° until hard, about 1 hour.

5 For the stems: wrap wire with florist tape. Stretch the tape for a snug fit.

6 Twist the end of the wire with needle-nose pliers to form a loop for the center of the flower.

7 Slip on the flower.

8 Tear off a 6″ length of floral tape and wrap under the flower to hold it in place.

Smiling Sun

Suns are fun to do. With minor facial changes a smiling summer sun can become a blowing autumn sun. The garlic press rays are time consuming to make, but they are worth the effort. For another effect, try making the sun out of yellow colored dough. Do not make the facial circle over 6″ in diameter, or later on it might crack. To protect the rays from breaking, the sun should be glued to a wooden plaque after it is baked.

YOU WILL NEED:

aluminum foil
cookie sheet
rolling pin
knife
garlic press
pop bottle cap
toothpaste cap
nutpick
small paint brush
unlined paper
egg yolk
water

½ batch of dough
will make 1 sun

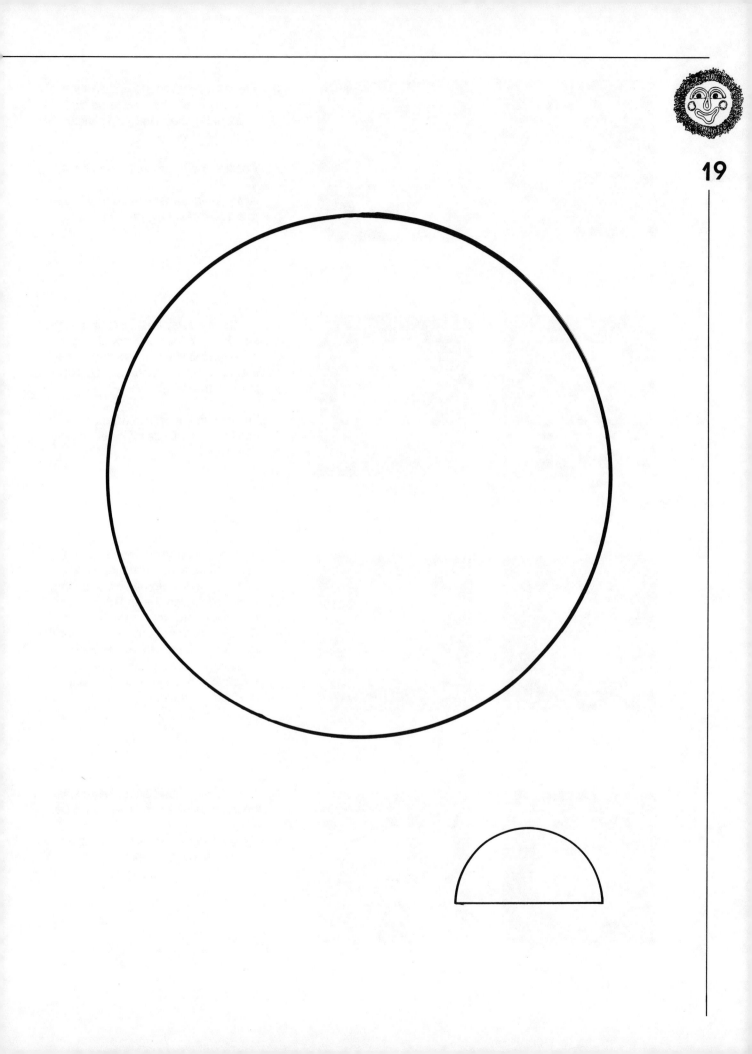

1 *2*

1 Trace the 2 sun shapes onto a sheet of unlined paper. Cut out 1 large circle and 2 half circles. Roll out a pancake of dough ¼" thick.

2 Position the large circle and cut out.

   At this point transfer the dough circle to a sheet of aluminum foil.

3 *4*

3 For the eyes: lay the half circles on the sun. Be sure to leave enough space between the eyes for the nose. Carefully cut around the shapes. Do not cut through the dough.

4 To finish the eyes: use a toothpaste cap to make a circle inside each of the half-circles.

5 *6*

5 For the nose and eyebrows: on the table roll a coil about 10" long and as thin as a pencil. Spread water on the underside of the coil and position on the face as shown.

6 For the mouth: roll out a second coil 6" long and as thin as a pencil. Join the ends together with water. Spread water on the underside of the coil and position as shown.

7 *8*

7 Form 2 very small balls of foil and place on the face where the cheeks will be.

8 Roll out dough ¼" thick and with a bottle cap cut out 2 cheeks.

9

10

11

12

A blowing sun

A sad sun

Cut out rays

Coiled rays

9 Put water on the back of the cheeks. Cover the foil and join to the face. With the blunt end of a nutpick make indentations around each cheek close to the edge.

10 For sun rays press dough through a garlic press and place around the edge of the face. This process takes some time. As you work, put water along the facial edge before positioning the rays.

11 A second row of rays is placed so that it folds back onto the first layer as shown. Be sure to join with water.

12 Brush eff yolk in the circles of the eyes. Bake at 325° until hard, about 3½ hours.

SUN VARIATIONS

By changing the shape of the mouth, eyebrows or rays you can create a totally different personality.

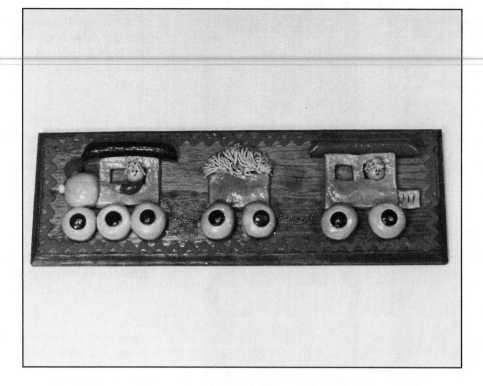

Little Locomotive

For your favorite engineer, here is a train made of simple dough shapes. After baking, paint the train as shown on the back of this book, or use your own color combinations. Then, with a fine-tipped black felt pen draw on the two faces. The three train pieces can be mounted on a long, narrow board (about 5″ by 15″), or on three small boards which would be hung in a line. In either case, a small chain or rope could be glued to attach the three cars to each other. For a circus train make the middle car a cage and add some "wild animals" inside.

YOU WILL NEED:

aluminum foil
cookie sheet
garlic press
lipstick cap
knife
rolling pin
ruler
water

½ batch of dough will make
1 little locomotive

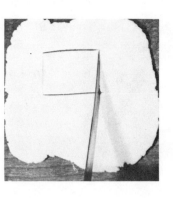

1

2

1 For the engine: roll out a pancake of dough ¼″ thick.

2 Cut a rectangle 2″ by 1½″.

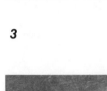

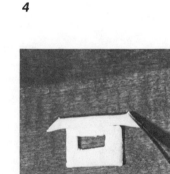

3

4

3 Toward the top of the rectangle cut a window 1″ by ½″.

At this point transfer the engine to a sheet of aluminum foil.

4 Roll a coil as thick as a pencil and at least 4″ long.

5

6

5 Spread water along the top of the rectangle then position the coil.

6 Cut the ends of the coil at an angle as shown. Leave about ½″ of the coil extending over each end of the rectangle.

7

8

7 Take a lump of dough about the size of an egg and roll it between your palms until smooth.

8 Place the ball on the table and flatten it with your fingers. Cut off one edge.

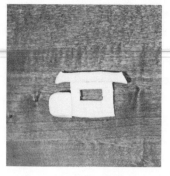

9

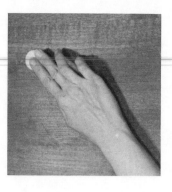

10

9 Spread water along the cut edge and attach to the rectangle.

10 For the wheels: take a lump of dough the size of a walnut and roll between your palms until smooth. Place the ball on the table and slightly flatten. Make 2 more wheels.

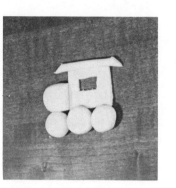

11

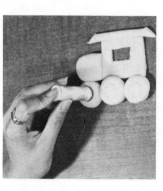

12

11 Position the wheels and join with water.

12 With a lipstick cap make a circle on each wheel.

13

14

13 For the engineer's arm: roll a coil as thin as a pencil. Cut to 1½". Pinch the cut end. Spread water along one side and place along the window.

14 For his head: roll a ball of dough the size of a grape. Moisten the back and place it inside the window. Fill a garlic press with dough and squeeze out ½" of dough. Put water on the head and arrange the hair.

15

16

15 For the smokestack: roll a bit of dough the size of a grape until smooth. Pinch one end while flattening the other end.

16 Place as shown and join with water.

17

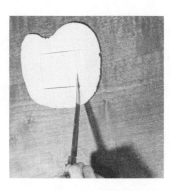

18

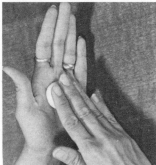

19

20

21

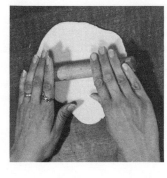

22

23

24

17 For the engine light: roll a tiny ball of dough and join with water to the front.

18 For the boxcar: roll out a pancake of dough ¼″ thick. Cut a rectangle 2½″ by 1″.

At this point transfer the rectangle to a sheet of aluminum foil.

19 Form 2 wheels each with a lump of dough the size of a walnut. Roll until smooth. Place on the table and slightly flatten.

20 Join the wheels to the bottom of the rectangle with water. Using the lipstick cap make a circle on each wheel.

21 For hay: fill a garlic press with dough. Spread water along the top of the box-car. Position the hay as shown.

22 For the caboose: roll out another pancake of dough ¼″ thick.

23 Cut a rectangle 2½″ by 1½″. Cut two windows each ¾″ by ½″.

At this point transfer the caboose to a sheet of aluminum foil.

24 Roll a coil as thick as a pencil and at least 4″ long.

25

26

25 Spread water along the top of the rectangle and position the coil.

26 Cut the ends of the coil at an angle as shown. Leave about ½″ of the coil extending over each end of the rectangle.

27

28

27 Make 2 wheels each with a lump of dough the size of a walnut. Roll until smooth and flatten slightly.

28 Join them with water to the bottom of the rectangle.

29

30

29 With the lipstick cap make a circular indentation on each wheel.

30 For the caboose platform: roll out a small pancake of dough ¼″ thick. Cut ½″ square. Attach with water as shown.

31

32

31 With a knife make 3 cuts in the square.

32 For the head: roll a ball of dough the size of a grape. Place it inside the window and join with water. Use a garlic press to make some hair and attach it with water.

Bake at 325° until hard, about 3 hrs.

Clown With Balloons

Clowns are bright and colorful and always popular. After baking, paint the clown's balloons to match a child's bedroom or use the primary colors of red, yellow, and blue. By changing his face and hairstyle, the clown can be turned into a little boy. Personalize him by making a dough football, basketball, ice cream cone, etc. Or, purchase a miniature item such as a fishing rod, tennis racquet, or puppy and glue on after baking. These items are available where doll house miniatures are sold.

YOU WILL NEED:

aluminum foil
cookie sheet
knife
rolling pin
nutpick
garlic press
ruler
water

½ batch of dough will make
2 clowns with balloons

1

1   For the head: take a lump of dough the size of a walnut. Roll it between your palms until smooth. Place on the table and gently flatten.

2   With the sharp end of a nutpick make a deep indentation for each eye.

At this point transfer the head to a sheet of aluminum foil.

2

3

3   Roll a ball the size of a pea and join with water to the face.

4   With a nut pick "stitch" on the mouth and eyebrows.

4

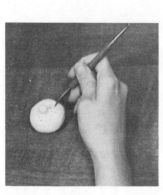

5

5   For the body: roll a lump of dough the size of a large egg between your palms until smooth. Pinch to form a teardrop shape.

6   Dip the narrow end of the body in water and place under the face.

6

7

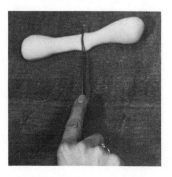

7   For the legs: roll a coil of dough 1" thick and 5" long. When smooth keep fingers in the middle and roll until each end is fatter.

8   Cut in half.

8

9

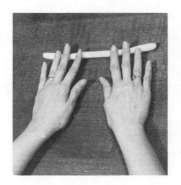

10

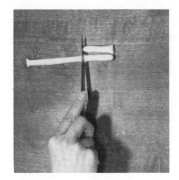

11

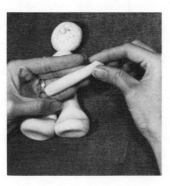

12

15

16

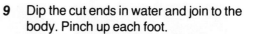

9 Dip the cut ends in water and join to the body. Pinch up each foot.

10 For the arms: roll a coil as thick as a pencil.

11 Cut two arms, each 3″ long. The rounded ends will be the hands.

12 Pinch the cut end of each arm.

13 Dip the pinched ends in water and position as shown. Curve one arm outward and press the end with your finger to form a hand.

14 For pants: roll out a pancake of dough about ¼″ thick.

15 Cut a pants shape 2½″ across the top, 4″ across the bottom, and 3″ long. Make the cut for his legs. Cut two strips ¼″ wide and 4″ long.

16 Spread water on the back of the pants and place on the clown. Be sure the pants cover the sides of the clown.

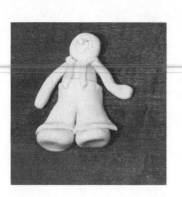

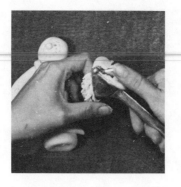

17 **18**

17 Dab water on each strip and position for suspenders. Cut off the excess.

18 For hair: fill a garlic press with dough and squeeze.

19 **20**

19 Put water on each side of the head and place the hair.

Bake at 325° until hard, about 3 hours.

20 For balloons: make a foil ball about the size of a walnut. Place on the table to flatten the back.

21 **22**

21 Roll out a pancake of dough about ¼" thick. Cover the foil form with the dough. Mold the dough around the form so its outline can be seen clearly.

22 Cut away the excess dough leaving ½" all around.

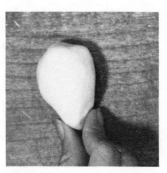

23 **24**

23 Press the ½" of dough around to the back of the foil.

24 Pinch one end to form a point. Transfer to a sheet of aluminum foil.

Bake at 325° until hard, about 2 hours.

Old-Fashioned Girl

For someone special here is an old-fashioned girl. She is a modification of the quilt pattern called "Sunbonnet Sue." To add color after she is baked, paint the apron and the strip on the bonnet. Sometimes during baking one or both feet will lift up — it usually presents no problem. If you like, draw on a face with a fine-tipped black felt pen. Seal the piece, then glue on a fabric bow at the back of the girl's apron. If your special person has a fondness for cats or dogs, you might buy a miniature one to glue in the girl's hands. She could also hold flowers or a basket. Whenever possible, it is nice to personalize the dough pieces.

YOU WILL NEED:

aluminum foil
cookie sheet
garlic press   1 batch of dough will bake
knife   6 old-fashioned girls
rolling pin
water

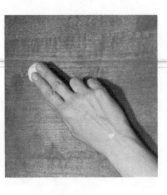

1

2

1 For the head: take a lump of dough the size of a walnut. Roll it between your palms until smooth.

2 Place the ball on a table and gently flatten.

At this point transfer the head to a sheet of aluminum foil.

3

4

3 For the hair: press dough through a garlic press. Moisten the back of the head with water and place the hair as shown.

4 Roll a ball of foil about the size of a walnut and place behind the head.

5

6

5 For the body: take a lump of dough about the size of a large egg. Roll between your palms until smooth.

6 Place the body on the table, flatten slightly and make a teardrop shape as pictured.

7

8

7 Dip the narrow end of the teardrop in water and place below the head.

8 For the legs: roll a coil as thick as a pencil. Cut each leg 2″ long. The rounded ends of the coil will become the feet.

9

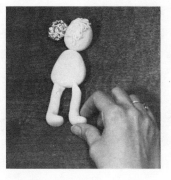

9 Shape each foot as shown.

10 Dip the cut end of each leg in water and join to the body.

10

11

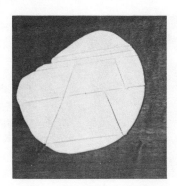

12

11 Roll out a pancake of dough ¼″ thick. For the dress cut a shape 3″ across the bottom, 2″ across the top and 2½″ long.

12 The apron is 3″ across the bottom, 2″ across the top, and 1½″ long. Cut 2 strips, each ¼″ wide and 3″ long.

13

14

13 Moisten the back of the dress and position on the body. Press the dress so it covers the sides of the body. Slightly flare out the hem.

14 Moisten the back of the apron with water and gather the 2″ top.

15

16

15 Arrange on the girl.

16 Moisten the back of one of the strips and place as shown.

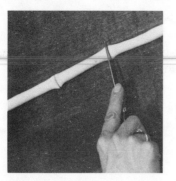

17

18

17 For the arms: roll a coil as thick as a pencil. Cut two pieces, each 2″ long. The rounded ends will be the hands.

18 Pinch the cut end. Spread water on one side of each arm and position as shown.

19

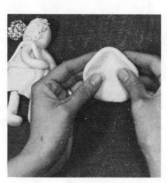

20

19 Moisten the back of the other strip and lay it across the arm from the apron to the back.

20 For the bonnet: take a lump of dough the size of a walnut. Roll between your palms until smooth. With your fingers work the dough until flat.

21

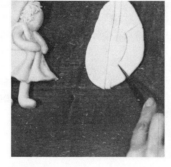

22

21 Place the bonnet over the foil so that no foil shows. Join with water where the bonnet meets the head.

22 Roll out a small pancake of dough ¼″ thick. Cut a strip ¼″ wide and 3″ long. Cut the hat brim 3″ along the outside edge, 2″ along the curved edge, and 1″ wide.

23

24

23 Moisten the back of the brim and position over the hair.

24 Put water on the back of the strip and position as shown. Cut off any excess. Bake at 325° until hard, about 3 hours.

Dried Flower Holders

Make these dried flower holders as plain or as fancy as you like. Use everyday items to create a variety of patterns on the holders. For instance, an open paper clip can be used to simulate feathers on the bird. A star cake decorating tip will add an interesting design to the pocket of the heart. After baking, paint the tail decorations on the bird and the ruffle on the heart to compliment the flowers you will use. Seal the dough, then glue in a small bouquet of dried flowers. Add a bit of baby's breath for a delicate look. A ribbon strung through the hook is a perfect finishing touch.

YOU WILL NEED:

aluminum foil
cookie sheet
pencil
unlined paper
scissors
nutpick
knife
paper clip or wire
rolling pin
peppercorn or clove
water

1 batch of dough will
make 6 dried flower holders

1

2

3

4

5

6

7

8

1 Trace the 2 heart shapes on a sheet of unlined paper and cut out. Roll out a pancake of dough ½″ thick. Position paper hearts and cut one of each size.

At this point transfer the large heart to a sheet of aluminum foil.

2 Moisten the back of the little heart with water. Position on the large heart. Pull the top of the little heart away, leaving a pocket.

3 Fill the pocket with a small piece of aluminum foil.

4 The blunt end of a nutpick makes a nice design around the little heart.

5 Roll out a large pancake of dough ¼″ thick. Cut as many ½″ wide strips as possible.

6 Gather each strip as shown. You may need to practice on a couple of strips before you have this technique perfected.

7 Moisten the outside edge of the heart with water and arrange the gathered strip. Repeat until the entire edge is covered.

8 For a hook: use a bent wire or half a paper clip. Insert into the heart as shown.

Bake at 325° until hard, about 3 hours. After baking remove the aluminum foil and glue in dried flowers.

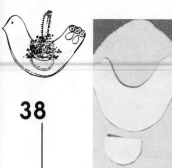

1

2

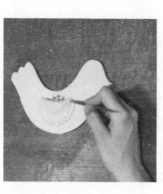

3

4

5

6

7

8

1 Trace the bird and wing pattern onto a sheet of unlined paper and cut out. Roll out a pancake of dough ½" thick. Position the paper patterns and cut out one of each.

At this point transfer the bird to a sheet of aluminum foil.

2 Moisten the back of the wing with water. Position on the bird. Pull the top of the wing away from the bird leaving a little pocket.

3 Fill the pocket with a small piece of aluminum foil.

4 Use the blunt end of a nutpick for a design around the wing.

5 Roll 3 balls, each the size of a pea, and join with water to the tail.

6 Make an indentation in the center of each ball with the blunt end of a nutpick.

7 Make 2 small flower petals and join with water on the tail. For the hook: use a bent wire or half a paper clip. Insert into the back of the bird.

8 Use a peppercorn or clove for the eye. Bake at 300° until hard, about 2 hours. After baking remove foil and glue in dried flowers.

The next five projects — mushroom house, teddy bear, rabbit, Mother Goose and rocking horse — use a form made of aluminum foil, which is then covered with dough. This foil form enables us to make larger, thicker dough art pieces without cracking.

1

1   Tear off a one foot length of aluminum foil, regular weight, twelve inches wide.

2

3

2   *Gently* shape the foil into a loose ball — not into a hard little one.

3   Put the foil on the table. Cup your hands as shown. Gently press the foil into a teardrop shape.

4   The shape should be narrow at the top and full at the bottom.

5   In this side view notice the slope of the foil. Try to match it. My foil forms are about 4″ long. At the widest section they are about 3″ across and 1½″ high.

4

5

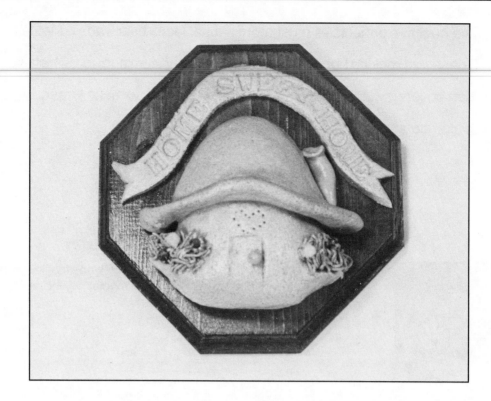

Home Sweet Home

This mushroom-like house is a favorite of mine. It would make a

delightful bridal shower or house warming gift. A rubber alphabet set

(found in toy departments) was used for the banner, but you could

"stitch" on the letters with a nutpick. The banner could also read "Bless

this house". Your own house numbers might replace the heart above

the door. Once baked, paint the grass and glue in a few dried flowers.

YOU WILL NEED:

aluminum foil
cookie sheet
rolling pin
knife
garlic press
nutpick
rubber alphabet set
water

1 batch of dough will
make 3 Home Sweet Homes

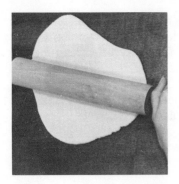

1

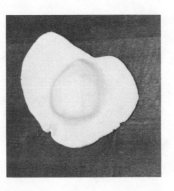

2

3

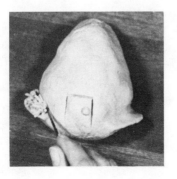

4

5

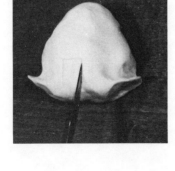

6

7

8

1 Make a foil form. Roll out a large pancake of dough about ¼″ thick.

2 Cover the foil form with the dough. Use your hands to press the dough around the form until its outline can be seen clearly.

3 Cut away the excess dough leaving ½″ around the form.

4 Pick up the form and press the extra dough around to the back.

At this point transfer the piece to a sheet of aluminum foil.

5 Pinch out a small ledge on each side of the base.

6 Cut a door, being sure not to go all the way through to the foil. Shape a small ball for the door knob. Put water on the back of the ball and place on the door.

7 For grass: fill the garlic press and squeeze out ½″ strands of dough. Scrape off the grass with a nutpick.

8 Dab water on the little ledges and place the grass. Several batches of grass may be needed.

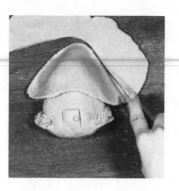

9

10

9 For the roof: roll out a pancake about ¼" thick and place it over the top of the house. Cut away the excess dough to form the roof.

10 Curve the edges up. Join to the house with water.

11

12

11 With a nutpick "stitch" a heart just above the door.

12 For the chimney: roll a coil ½" thick. Pinch out a ridge near one rounded end.

13

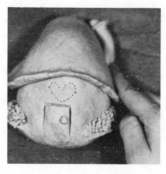

14

13 Make a diagonal cut leaving the chimney 2" long.

14 Spread water down one side of the chimney and join it to the house.

15

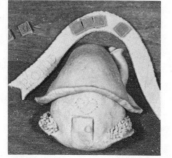

16

15 For the banner: roll out a pancake of dough ¼" thick. Cut a 1" wide curved strip as shown. Cut the ends as shown and place above the house.

16 For "Home Sweet Home" use a rubber stamp set to press in the letters or "stitch" on the letters with a nutpick just as you "stitched" on the heart.

Bake at 325° until hard — the banner will take about 1 hour and the house about 3 hours.

Teddy Bear

Teddy bears are great for either boys or girls. So, this bear would be a good choice for a baby shower gift. After he is baked, glue the bear, honey pot, and bees to a large wooden board. For color, glue rick rack around the edge of the board, and glue a matching ribbon at the bear's neck. Since this bear can sit, he could be glued to one end of a pair of wooden bookends. Glue the honey pot and bees to the other end. If you would like to experiment, try making a panda bear, a Winnie-the-Pooh type bear, a Paddington bear, or Goldilocks' three bears. There are many possibilities!

YOU WILL NEED:

aluminum foil
cookie sheet
rolling pin
nutpick
straw
knife
paint brush
rubber alphabet set
egg yolk
water

½ batch of dough will
make 1 teddy bear

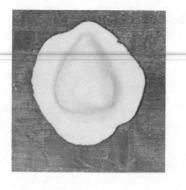

1   Make a foil form. Roll out a pancake of dough ¼″ thick.

2   Cover the foil form with the dough. Use your hands to mold the dough around the foil form, so its outline can be seen clearly.

1   *2*

3   Cut away the excess dough leaving ½″ all around the form.

4   Pick up the form and press the extra dough around to the back — this will be the bear's body.

At this point transfer the bear's body to a sheet of aluminum foil.

3   *4*

5   For the bear's head: take a lump of dough about the size of a tennis ball. Roll it between your palms until smooth. Turn any cracks to the back of the head.

6   Place the head next to the body and gently flatten the face. Pick up the body, dip the neck in water, and join to the head.

5   *6*

7   With a sharp knife cut a straight line down the center of the bear. Begin at the very top of the head and go to the end of the body. Do not cut all the way through to the foil.

8   With a straw make the eyes, notice they are quite close to the center line.

7   *8*

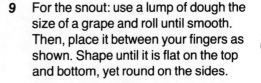

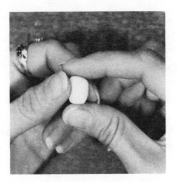

9

10

9 For the snout: use a lump of dough the size of a grape and roll until smooth. Then, place it between your fingers as shown. Shape until it is flat on the top and bottom, yet round on the sides.

10 Join the snout to the face with a drop of water. Make a very small ball for the nose. Position it as shown and join with water. Use a nutpick to "stitch" on the mouth.

11

12

11 For each ear: take a lump of dough the size of a grape. Roll it between your palms until smooth.

12 With the blunt end of a nutpick make an indentation in each ear as shown. Moisten with water and join the ears to the head.

13

14

13 For the cheeks: roll out a small pancake of dough ⅛" thick. Cut out 2 circles with a straw. If the dough sticks, gently blow from the other end of the straw and it will pop out.

14 Put a drop of water on the back of each cheek. Position on the face as shown.

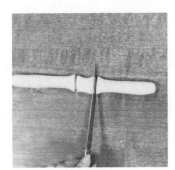

15

16

15 For the arms: roll a coil of dough as thick as your first finger. Cut 2 arms, each 3" long. The rounded ends of the coil will be the paws.

16 Pinch the cut end of each arm. Spread water down the length of each arm. Join onto the body with the pinched end at the neck. Curve the arms onto the tummy.

17

18

17 For the legs: roll another coil, fatter than the arms. Cut 2 legs, each 3″ long. The rounded ends of the coil will be the feet. Pinch the cut ends as shown. Moisten one entire side of each leg and join to the lowest part of the body.

18 For the feet: pinch the end of each leg as shown.

19

20

19 Use a straw to press a circle on the bottom of each foot to make the pads which all bears have.

20 With the blunt end of a nut pick, make 3 dots above each pad for toes.

21

22

21 Use the pointed end of a nutpick to make "stitches" along both sides of the center line. Cut a line down each arm and leg. Make "stitches" along both sides of each line.

22 Paint egg yolk in each eye. Bake at 325° until hard, about 3½ hours.

1

2

1 For the honey pot: start with a lump of dough the size of an egg. Roll between your palms to make it round and smooth.

2 For the lip of the honey pot: pinch an edge around the top of the ball.

3

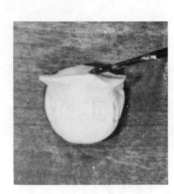

4

3 With a rubber stamp set press in HONEY. Or, stitch on HONEY with a nutpick.

4 Paint egg yolk on the top of the pot. Bake at 325° for about 3 hours, until hard.

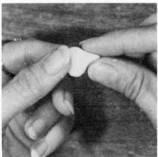

5

6

5 For honey bees: begin with a lump of dough about the size of a grape. Roll it into a ball and pinch one end which will be the head.

6 For strips on the honey bees: cut 3 lines on the back.

7

8

7 For each wing: take a small piece of dough and roll into a ball. Flatten the ball and pinch one end as shown. Moisten the wing. Place the pinched end of the wing next to the pinched end of the body.

8 For the head: roll a small ball, moisten with water, and join as pictured. Bake at 325° for about one hour.

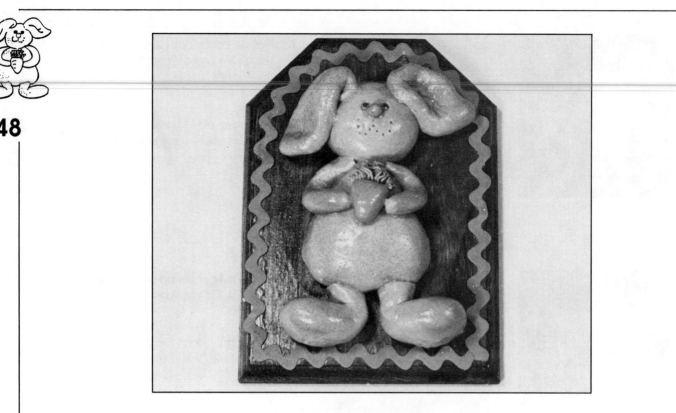

Rabbit

What's up Doc? This likable little rabbit! He would be right at home in any child's bedroom. If you choose to add the carrot, paint it after the rabbit is baked. If made as an Easter bunny, do not add the carrot. Instead, glue a jelly bean or a small basket between his paws after baking. Rabbits are everywhere! For other designs look in coloring books or children's magazines. You might like to make your own dough version of Bugs Bunny, Peter Rabbit, or the very special bunny in the book *Velveteen Rabbit*.

YOU WILL NEED:

aluminum foil
cookie sheet
knife
straw
rolling pin
nutpick
garlic press
egg yolk
small paint brush
water

½ batch of dough
will make 1 rabbit

1

2

3

4

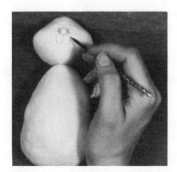

5

6

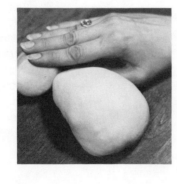

7

8

1 Make a foil form. Roll out a pancake of dough ¼″ thick.

2 Cover the foil form with the dough. Press the dough around the form until you can see its outline clearly.

3 Cut away the excess dough leaving ½″ of dough around the body.

4 Press the ½″ of dough around to the back of the form.

At this point transfer the body to a sheet of aluminum foil.

5 For the head: take a lump of dough the size of a tennis ball. Work it until smooth. Form it into a diamond shape by holding the top of the ball in your palm and rolling the under half on the table.

6 Flatten the head just a bit. Join it to the body with water.

7 With the end of a straw make 2 eyes (they are very close together). Make a small ball for the nose and join with water. With the sharp end of a nutpick "stitch" on the mouth.

8 For 1 ear: roll a coil of dough about 4″ long and 1″ thick.

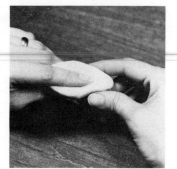

9

10

9 Press a groove into the center of the ear. The rounded end of the ear (on the right) should be pinched to a slight point. Flatten the other end.

10 Put water on the flattened end and join to the head just above one of the eyes.

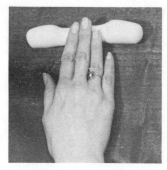

11

12

11 Make a second ear and join with water. Flip the end of this ear over.

12 For the arms roll a coil as thick as your first finger. Cut so each arm is 3″ long. The rounded ends will be the paws.

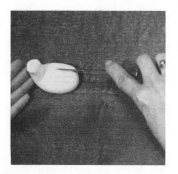

13 Pinch the cut ends. Spread water down the length of each arm. Join onto the body with the pinched end at the neck. Curve the arms onto the tummy.

14 For big jack rabbit feet: roll a coil 1″ thick and 4″ long. When smooth keep fingers in the middle and roll until each end is fatter. Cut in half.

13

14

15 Stand each foot as shown. Make 3 indentations for toes.

16 Join the feet to the body with water. Paint egg yolk in the eyes. Bake at 325° until hard, about 3 hours.

* OPTIONAL CARROT: use a small ball of dough. Pinch one end and flatten the other. Join to the body with water. Use dough squeezed through a garlic press for the carrot top.

15

16

Mother Goose

Mother Goose is a natural addition to any nursery. To give her some color after baking, glue a fabric bow at the neck and paint her kerchief a matching shade. The book she holds is easily made from pieces of paper cut to measure 1″ by 2″. Fold and staple the book together. Print *Stories by Mother Goose* on the cover. After you have sealed the dough, glue the book between her wings.

YOU WILL NEED:

aluminum foil
cookie sheet
rolling pin
straw
knife
garlic press
small paint brush
egg yolk
water

½ batch of dough will
make 1 Mother Goose

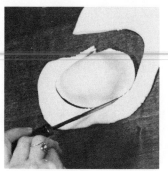

1

2

3

4

5

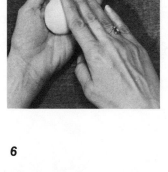

7

8

1 For the body: make a foil form. Roll out a pancake of dough ¼″ thick. Cover the foil form with dough and press the dough around the form. Cut away the excess dough leaving ½″ all around the form.

2 Pick up the form and press the extra dough around to the back.

At this point transfer the body to a sheet of aluminum foil.

3 Turn the body as shown and pinch up the tail feathers.

4 For the neck: roll a coil of dough 1″ thick. Cut a piece 1″ long.

5 Dampen one cut end with water and attach it to the body as shown.

6 For the head: roll until smooth a ball of dough the size of an egg.

7 Dampen the other end of the neck and attach the head.

8 The beak is a small ball of dough ½″ in diameter. Roll until smooth and place it between your fingers as shown. Pinch one end and flatten the other.

9

10

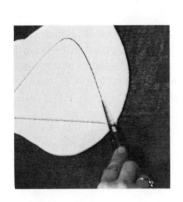

11

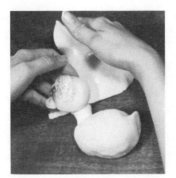

12

13

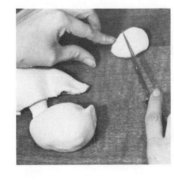

14

15

16

9 Attach the beak with water. Using a knife, press in a line along the beak. For the hair: squeeze dough through a garlic press. Position it as shown and join with water.

10 Use a straw to make an indentation for the eye — only one eye is needed.

11 For the kerchief: roll out a pancake of dough ⅛″ thick. Cut a triangle 6″ by 5″ by 5″.

12 Dampen the top surface of the kerchief. Lift the head and slide half the kerchief under. Keep the dampened side next to the head. Lower the head and bring the kerchief down onto the face.

13 For the cheek: flatten a small piece of dough until it is ⅛″ thick. Use a straw to cut out the cheek. Put water on the back of the cheek and place on the face.

14 For the right wing: roll out a pancake of dough ¼″ thick. Cut a triangle 1″ by 1″ by 1″.

15 Spread water on one edge of the triangle and join it to the body.

16 Put a small ball of foil on top of the wing.

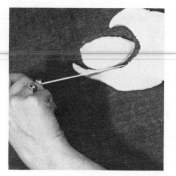

17

18

17 For the left wing: roll out another pancake of dough ¼" thick. Cut an oval 3½" long by 2" wide.

18 Spread water on the back of the wing and place it on the body. Be sure it covers the foil ball. Pinch the end of the wing up to a slight point.

19

20

19 For the feet: roll a coil 1" thick and at least 4" long. When smooth keep fingers in the middle and roll until each end is fatter. Cut in half.

20 Stand up one foot as shown.

21

22

21 Cut out webbed toes.

22 Dip the cut end of the leg in water and join it to the body.

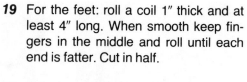

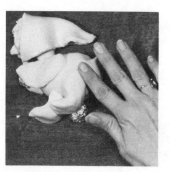

23

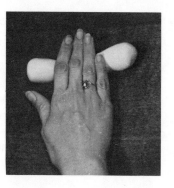

24

23 Place a ball of foil behind the first foot.

24 Cut the toes for the second foot. Dip the cut end in water, and place the second foot over the foil. Smooth the top of the leg onto the body. Paint egg yolk in the eye.

Bake at 350° until hard, about 3 hours. After baking remove both foil balls.

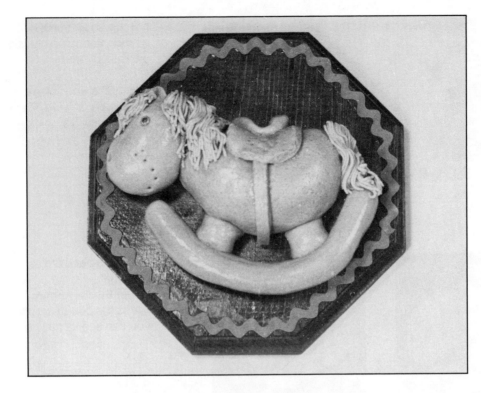

Rocking Horse

Modeled after an old-fashioned toy, this rocking horse would be appropriate for any boy or girl. To add some color after he is baked, you could paint the blanket. Or, if you glue the horse to a wooden plaque, also glue rick rack to the outside edge of the board. To make him an Appaloosa rocking horse, before baking paint splotches of egg yolk or egg white on the horse's body. If there is a cowboy in your life, make this rocking horse with a cowboy on his back. Follow the instructions for making a clown, but change the face and hair. Another variation would be to make the horse 2″ tall for a charming Christmas tree ornament.

YOU WILL NEED:

aluminum foil
cookie sheet
rolling pin
knife
nut pick
straw
garlic press
small paint brush
egg yolk
water

1 batch of dough will
make 3 rocking horses

56

1

2

1 For the body: make a foil form. Press an indentation on one side — the saddle will go there.

2 Round the ends of the foil form so it is 3″ long and 2″ wide. Press the top down so the body is 1″ thick.

3

4

3 Roll out a pancake of dough ¼″ thick.

4 Cover the foil form with the dough. Press the dough around the form until you can see its outline clearly.

5

6

5 Cut away the excess dough leaving ½″ around the form.

6 Pick up the form and press the extra dough around to the back.

At this point transfer the piece to a sheet of aluminum foil.

7

8

7 For the head: use a lump of dough the size of a large egg. Roll it until smooth. Form an oval and join it to the body with water.

8 With your knuckle make an indentation in the middle of the head to form the horse's nose.

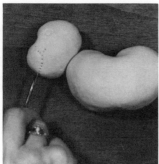

9

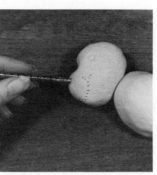

10

9 For the eye: make an indentation with the end of a straw. Use the sharp end of a nutpick to "stitch" on the mouth. Be sure the stitches at the end form a V.

10 With the blunt end of the nutpick make two indentations for the nostrils.

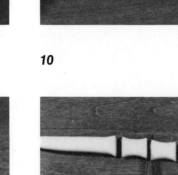

11

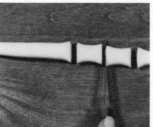

12

11 Pinch up an ear: one is all you need.

12 For legs: roll a coil ½" thick. Cut two pieces, each ½" long.

13

14

13 Moisten one end of each leg and join to the horse's body.

14 For the rocker: roll a coil ½" thick. It should measure about 7" long.

15

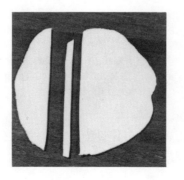

16

15 Position the rocker and trim off any excess length. Round the cut ends with water. Join to the legs with water.

16 Roll out a pancake of dough ¼" thick. Cut a strip ¼" wide and 4" long.

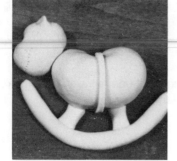

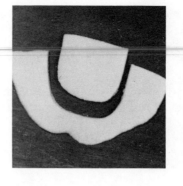

17

18

17 Moisten the back of the strip with water and join to the horse's body.

18 Roll out another pancake of dough ¼" thick. Cut out the blanket shape as shown. It should measure about 1½" wide and 2" long.

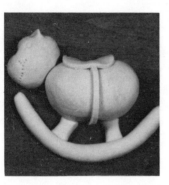

19

20

19 Put water on the back of the blanket and position as shown.

20 The saddle is a 1" long coil. Squeeze it in the middle and join it to the blanket with water.

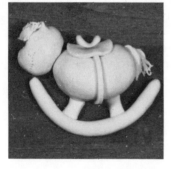

21

22

21 For the mane and tail: squeeze dough through a garlic press. Position as shown and join with water.

22 When finishing the mane, notice that the dough comes toward the face.

23

24

23 With a sharp end of a nutpick "stitch" a heart on the blanket.

24 Paint egg yolk on the eye. Bake at 325° until hard, about 3 hours.

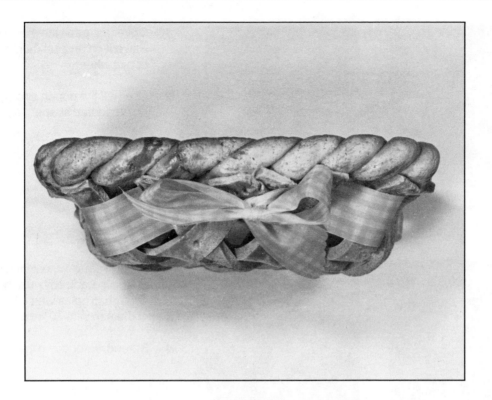

Bread Baskets

Dough bread baskets were one of the first dough art projects to become popular. They are not difficult to make, but there is a trick in baking — lower the oven temperature to 275°, and bake 6 to 8 hours. Also, you must allow the basket to cool slowly. When the dough is completely hard, either turn off the oven and allow the basket to cool, or remove the basket from the oven and wrap it in towels. There is no need for your dough baskets to hold only rolls and breads. Fill a basket with jars of homemade jam, or use your basket as a container for a dried flower arrangement, or as a unique Easter or May Day basket. Seal the basket with several coats of Varathane or a similar protective medium.

YOU WILL NEED:

aluminum foil
cookie sheet
knife
fork   1 batch of dough will
nutpick   make 1 bread basket
pan about 8½″ by 4½″ by 2½″
egg white
water

1

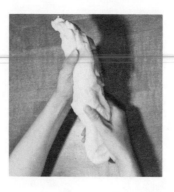

2

1. Cover the pan with aluminum foil. Place it on an aluminum foil covered cookie sheet.

2. Use half the dough and squeeze it into an elongated shape.

3

4

3. Roll the dough into 2 long coils, each ¾″ thick. Each coil must be long enough to go around the outside edge of the pan with 10″ extra.

4. Spread water down both coils.

5

6

5. Twist the coils together. Be careful not to pull the coils for they will stretch and break.

6. Place the coils around the edge of the pan. Avoid pressing the coils into the lip of the pan. Note: if your pan has handles, be sure to lay the coils around the handles and not over them.

7

8

7. Cut off the extra dough where the ends of the coils meet.

8. Separate the 4 ends and join with water so that the break is as smooth as possible.

9

10

11

12

13

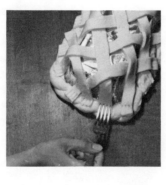

14

15

16

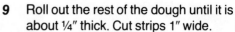

9 Roll out the rest of the dough until it is about ¼" thick. Cut strips 1" wide.

10 Lay 4 strips as shown.

11 Weave another strip in and out. Join with water wherever dough touches dough. Do nothing with the ends.

12 Weave the remaining 3 strips as shown. Join with water.

13 Cut off the strip ends to be even with the outside edge of the coils. Lift each end, dab the underside with water, and place on the coil.

14 Press with a fork, as shown.

15 Use the blunt end of a nutpick to press the strips wherever they cross.

16 Spread egg white on the dough. Bake at 250° until hard, about 6-8 hours. Allow the basket to cool slowly either in the oven or wrapped in towels.

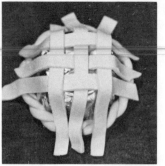

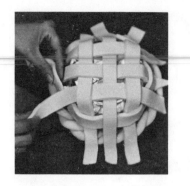

17 For a round pan: weave the strips as shown joining with water.

18 Weave a strip along the side to strengthen the basket. It may take several strips to weave this 1 long strip. Be sure to join with water as you go.

17   *18*

Use a cookie cutter for another type of basket. Keep in mind this basket is a bit more fragile.

19 Roll out a pancake of dough ¼" thick.

20 Use the cookie cutter to cut as many shapes as possible.

19   *20*

21 Place the first flowers as shown — join with water.

22 Around the edge place the next row of flowers and join with water. Do not have any petals laying on the cookie sheet because after baking they are extremely fragile.

21   *22*

23 Continue adding flowers until the pan is covered. Remember to join with water.

24 Press the blunt end of a nutpick into the center of each flower. Spread egg white on the flowers. Bake at 250° until hard, about 4 hours. Allow to cool slowly.

23   *24*

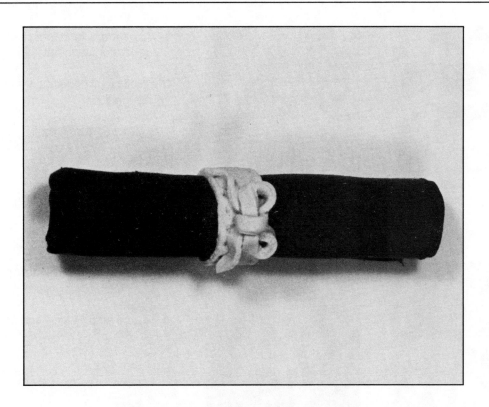

Napkin Rings

While napkin rings may not be used with your everyday meals, they do add a festive touch on holidays and special occasions. The napkin ring pictured above would be appropriate for a birthday or anniversary dinner. You could make the bow out of colored dough to match your tablecloth or dishes. A few sprigs of dried baby's breath, glued under the bow, would be a nice touch. For Halloween make a little dough pumpkin instead of the bow. Use a fine-tipped black felt pen to draw on a jack-o-lantern's face. For sturdier napkin rings, braid coils of dough around a cardboard for tube like a Christmas wreath. After dinner let each guest take a napkin ring home. You can easily make more for the next time!

YOU WILL NEED:
aluminum foil
cookie sheet
rolling pin
knife
cardboard tube from toilet paper
star cake decorating tube
water

½ batch of dough will
make 12 napkin rings

1

2

3

4

5

6

7

8

1 Cover a toilet paper cardboard tube with aluminum foil.

2 Roll a coil of dough about 1″ thick and 5″ long.

3 With a rolling pin flatten the coil until it is ½″ thick.

4 Cut a strip 1″ wide and 5″ long.

5 With a fork make indentations along both edges of the strip.

6 With a cake decorating tube press a design along the center of the strip.

7 Wrap the strip around the aluminum covered tube.

8 Cut off the excess dough so there is no overlapping.

9 Join the cut ends with water.

10 Turn the tube over so the cut ends are hidden.

At this point transfer the tube to a sheet of aluminum foil.

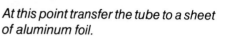

9 *10*

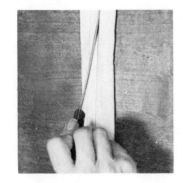

11 For the bow: roll a coil of dough. With a rolling pin flatten the coil until it is ¼″ thick. Cut a strip ¼″ wide and 10″ long.

12 Cut a 2″ piece off the end of the strip. Save this for step 16.

11 *12*

13 Grasp both ends of the strip.

14 Bring the ends around on top of the center of the strip.

13 *14*

15 Moisten the bow. Flip it over and place it on the napkin ring.

16 Cut the ends of the bow to the length pictured. Take the short 2″ strip from step 12. Dab water on the back of the strip and place it on the center of the bow. Curve it around.

Bake at 250° until hard, about 3 hours.

15 *16*

Jar Lid Covers

Fast and easy — dough jar lid covers are fun to make. There are many possibilities for decorating the tops of the lids. Let the contents of the jar spark your imagination. The rose lid would be nice on a jar of potpourri. How about a teddy bear on a jar of honey? Or, you can glue small items onto a plain baked lid — pine cones, hard candy, or buttons are some things you might try. Since the lids are to be handled quite a bit, seal them with Varathane or a similar protective medium.

YOU WILL NEED:

*aluminum foil
cookie sheet
knife
rolling pin
jar lid
lipstick cap
water*

½ batch of dough will
make 6 jar lid covers

1   Roll out a pancake of dough ¼″ thick.

2   Cover the jar lid with the dough. Press the dough around the lid. Cut off the excess dough.

1

2

3   Smooth the cut edge. Be sure none of the dough is under or inside the jar lid.

4   With a table knife make lines (not cuts) around the side of the lid every ½″ or so.

3

4

5   Use a lipstick cap to make a circle between each of the knife lines.

6   For the rose: roll a coil of dough about ½″ thick and 6″ long. With a rolling pin flatten the coil until ⅛″ thick.

5

6

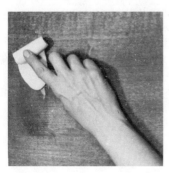

7   Spread some water down the center of the dough. Roll up the dough as shown.

8   The end of the roll should look like this.

7

8

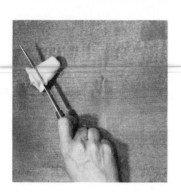

9

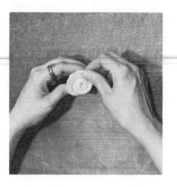

10

9 Pinch and fan out the layers of dough to form a rose.

10 Cut the rose as short as possible.

11

12

11 Put water on the jar lid and attach the rose.

12 For the leaves: roll until smooth a lump of dough the size of a grape. Flatten the ball between your fingers. Pinch one end as shown.

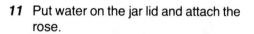

13

14

13 With a sharp knife make small cuts into the leaf edges.

14 Make the center line. *Do not* cut through the leaf.

15

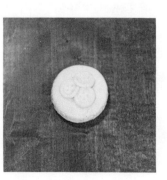

16

15 Make three leaves and join with water as shown.

  Bake at 250° until hard, about 4 hours.

16 Another idea is to make dough buttons for that jar full of loose buttons.

This section of the book is devoted to Christmas ornaments. These ornaments have proven to be successful projects with children. Even first grade youngsters with supervision can make an attractive "JOY." For the braided wreath, young children should twist two coils of dough together, rather than braid three coils. The angel, elf, and dove are better suited for older children, third grade and up. Since Christmas ornaments are stored away most of the year in hot attics, damp basements, or unheated garages, it is very important that the pieces be thoroughly sealed. Use Varathane or a polymer coating such as Decopour. Even clear fingernail polish will do. Shellac yellows after a time, so do not use it. A gloss finish looks best.

YOU WILL NEED:

for the JOY:
aluminum foil
cookie sheet
rolling pin
unlined paper
scissors
wire or paper clip
knife
water

for the wreath:
aluminum foil
cookie sheet
wire or paper clip
sesame seeds
egg white
water

½ batch of dough will
make 10 JOYs or 4 wreaths

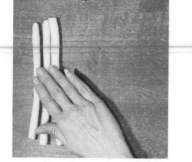

1

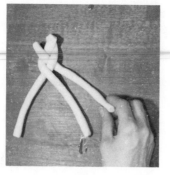

2

3

4

5

6

7

8

For the wreath:

1 Roll 3 coils of dough each as thick as a pencil and each 7" long. Spread water down each coil.

2 Braid the coils as tightly as possible. To braid — lift the right coil and place it between the other two, then lift the left coil and place between the other two.

3 Repeat until the piece is completely braided.

4 Cut off each end. Moisten the cut ends with water. Keeping the braid on the table, curve the ends around until they meet.

5 Spread egg white on top of the braid.

6 Sprinkle on sesame seeds or poppy seeds.

At this point transfer the wreath to a sheet of aluminum foil.

7 For the hook: use a bent wire or half a paper clip. Insert into the wreath where the ends meet.

Bake at 325° until hard, about 2½ hours.

8 After baking seal with acrylic spray. Cut a 14" length of gingham ribbon and thread through the hook. Pull all but 6" through the hook.

9

9   Bring the long end of the ribbon around to the back of the wreath then up through the center hole. Tie.

10 Make a bow.

10

1

2

1   Trace the JOY pattern onto a sheet of unlined paper and cut out. Roll out a pancake of dough ¼″ thick. Position the paper pattern and cut.

2   Dip your finger in water and smooth the cut edges.

   At this point transfer the JOY onto a sheet of aluminum foil.

3

4

3   With a knife outline the letter O. Do not cut completely through the dough.

4   For the hook: use a bent wire or half a paper clip. Insert into the Joy O.

   Bake at 300° until hard, about 1½ hours.

5

6

TWO JOY VARIATIONS:

5   After baking, seal the dough with acrylic spray. Then place the JOY on a piece of aluminum foil. Take a small bunch of red dried flowers and cut the stems to ½″. Dip the stems in craft glue and place in the O. Allow to dry 24 hours. Peal off the foil.

6   Plastic cooking crystals can be added to the dough just before baking. Fill the O with crystals and bake as usual.

Christmas Angel

After making the basic angel you can create many variations. Make an angel holding a lollipop, with praying hands, or holding a songbook. You might like to change the dress by adding a collar, a pocket, some "stitches" along the hem, or a ruffle. Try different hair styles by making braids, long flowing hair, short curly hair, or ponytails. Change the hair and skin color by using colored dough or by painting the angel. Once baked, use a fine-tipped black felt pen to draw on her face. Paint the dress and sleeves (not the hands) a bright color. Your angel could also be used on a package to hold a piece of paper reading "TO_____FROM_____".

YOU WILL NEED:

aluminum foil
cookie sheet
garlic press
knife
rolling pin   ½ batch will make 5 angels
fork
wire or paper clip
water

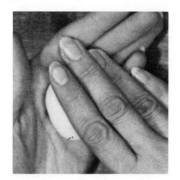

1

2

1. For the body: take a lump of dough the size of an egg and roll until smooth.

2. Place on the table and flatten with your fingers until about ½″ thick. Shape the top as shown.

   At this point transfer the body onto a sheet of aluminum foil.

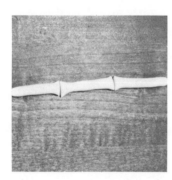

3

4

3. For the head: use a lump of dough a little smaller than for the body. Roll until smooth. Gently flatten with your fingers until ½″ thick.

4. Join with water to the body.

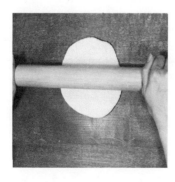

5

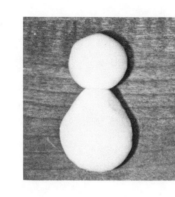

6

5. For the legs: roll a coil of dough as thick as a pencil. Cut each leg 2″ long. The rounded ends should be the feet.

6. Join with water to the body.

7

8

7. Roll out a pancake of dough ¼″ thick.

8. Cut out the dress. Note the top is narrower than the hem. The dress should reach from her neck to just over the top of her legs. Also, be sure the dress covers her sides.

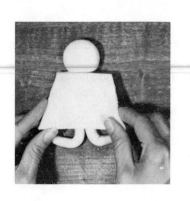

9

10

9   Test the dress on the angel to be sure it fits — if not, trim or re-roll and cut.

10   When the dress fits, join with water.

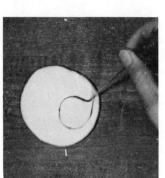

11

12

11   For the first wing: roll out a pancake of dough ¼″ thick. Cut a leaf shape as shown.

12   Use the first wing as a pattern for the second wing. Simply cut around it.

13

14

13   Dip the rounded end of each wing in water and join to the angel as shown.

14   For the arms: roll out a coil of dough as thin as a pencil. Cut each arm about 1½″ long. The rounded ends will be the hands.

15

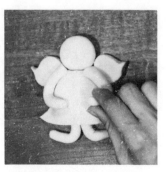

16

15   Flatten the cut ends. Spread water down one side of each arm.

16   Curve each arm onto her body.

17

18

17 For the hair: spread water around the edge of the head. Fill a garlic press with dough and squeeze out 1″. Lay the hair on one side of her head.

18 Fill the garlic press again and squeeze out another 1″ of dough. Place on the other side of her head.

19

20

19 Fill the garlic press once again and squeeze out 1″ of dough. Place on the top of the head and bring forward onto her face.

20 For the hook: form the wire into a U shape or use half a paper clip. Insert into the head.

21

22

21 Use the ends of a fork to make a design on the wing tips.

ANGEL VARIATIONS TO BE DONE BEFORE BAKING:

22 The hands can be brought together and pinched up to form praying hands.

23 For a lollipop: break a toothpick in half and insert one piece into the angel's hand. Stick a ball of dough on the other end. After baking paint a swirl on the lollipop.

24 A songbook is made from a pancake of dough ⅛″ thick and pinched in the middle. Join with water to the angel.

Bake at 325° until hard, about 3 hours.

23

24

Elf

This impish elf is very easy to make. After he is baked paint on his pants, boots, and shirt. Seal with several coats of Varathane or a similar product. For the belt cut a strip of black electrical tape. And for the belt buckle use a piece of gold tape. A small bell or pom pom glued to the tip of his hat would finish him nicely. Just like the Christmas angel, your elf can be used as a Christmas tree ornament or as a package tie.

YOU WILL NEED:

aluminum foil
cookie sheet
nutpick
garlic press
straw
knife
water

½ batch of dough
will make 5 elves

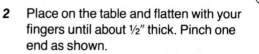

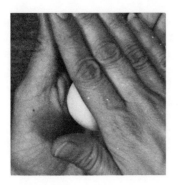

1

2

1 For the body: take a lump of dough the size of an egg and roll between your palms until smooth.

2 Place on the table and flatten with your fingers until about ½″ thick. Pinch one end as shown.

At this point transfer the body onto a sheet of aluminum foil.

3

4

3 For the head: use a lump of dough a little smaller than for the body. Roll it until smooth, and place on the table and flatten until ½″ thick. Join with water to the body.

4 With the blunt end of a nutpick make two impressions for the eyes.

5

6

5 For the mouth: cut the straw as illustrated. Use the straw to make the elf's smile.

6 Make a tiny ball for the nose and join it to the face with water.

7

8

7 For the legs: roll a coil of dough as thick as a pencil. Cut each leg 2″ long. The rounded ends will be the feet.

8 Join the legs to the body with water.

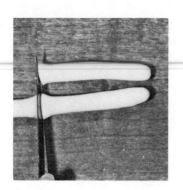

9

10

9 For the arms: roll out a coil of dough as thin as a pencil. Cut each arm about 1½″ long. The rounded ends will be the hands.

10 Pinch each cut end.

11

12

11 Spread water down one side of each arm. Curve the arms onto his tummy.

12 For the ears: roll a tiny ball of dough until smooth. Pinch one end.

13

14

13 Dab a bit of water on the head and place each ear. With the blunt end of a nutpick gently make an indentation in the ear.

14 For hair: fill a garlic press with dough. Spread water on the top of the head. Squeeze the press until 1½″ of dough comes out. Arrange the hair on the elf.

15

16

15 For the hat: take a lump of dough the size of a walnut and roll it smooth. Press it down over your knuckle.

16 Dab water on the hair and place the hat. Curve the end to one side. Insert a wire hook.

Bake at 325° until hard, about 3 hours.

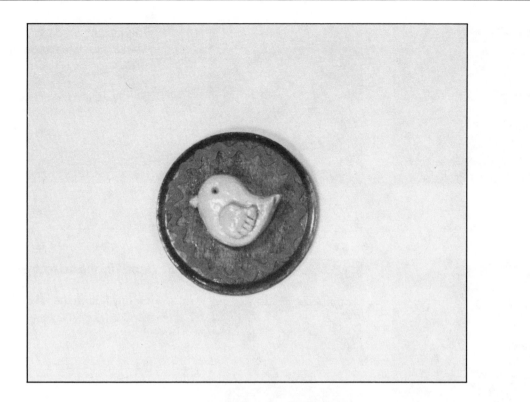

Dove

In making this little dove you will be working with tiny pieces of dough, so a bit of patience will be required. However, the dove is very quick to make. For a variation you could color the dough blue. If used as a Christmas tree ornament seal with several coats of Varathane or a similar product. Then glue a sprig of holly at the beak. A red ribbon strung through the wire hook would brighten up this fellow. Several doves can be hung for a mobile. Or, bake the dove without a hook, glue him to a small round board, and hang on the wall as a year-round symbol of peace.

YOU WILL NEED:

aluminum foil
cookie sheet
nutpick
knife
wire
water

¼ batch of dough
will make 9 doves

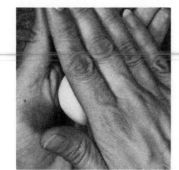

1

2

1   Take a lump of dough the size of a walnut. Roll it between your palms until smooth.

2   Gently flatten the dough until ½" thick.

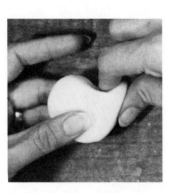

3

4

3   Pinch up the tail feathers.

4   Gently flatten the head.

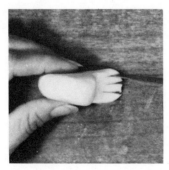

5

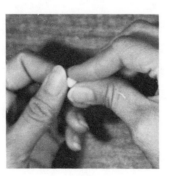

6

5   Make an indentation for the back.

6   Your dove should look like this.

   At this point transfer the dove to a sheet of aluminum foil.

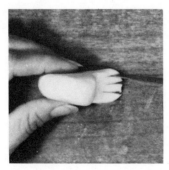

7

8

7   Pick up and make 3 cuts for the tail feathers.

8   For the beak: roll a tiny ball of dough until smooth. Pinch one side as shown.

9

10

11

12

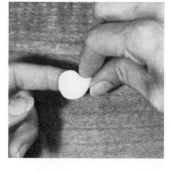

13

14

15

16

9   Join the beak to the head with water.

10 With a knife press a line along the beak.

11 Make an eye with the blunt end of a nutpick.

12 With the sharp end of a nutpick, make the center of the eye.

13 For the wing: take a bit of dough the size of a grape, and roll until smooth.

14 Cut in feathers.

15 Dab water on the back of the wing and place on the dove.

16 Insert a wire hook into the back of the dove. Bake at 325° until hard, about 1 hour. Seal.

Letters

Here are three sets of letters — two types of capitals and one in lower case. The cover of this book shows a fourth style of letters using coiled dough. These letters will help you to personalize your projects. Following the instructions there are some suggestions for using the letters.

YOU WILL NEED:

aluminum foil
cookie sheet
knife
unlined paper
pencil
scissors

½ batch of dough will make
about 20 capital letters

1

2

1 Trace the letters you will need on a sheet of unlined paper and cut them out.

2 Roll out a pancake of dough ¼" thick.

3

4

3 Place the letters and use a sharp knife to cut out.

At this point transfer the letters onto a sheet of aluminum foil.

4 Dip your finger in water and smooth the cut edges. Bake at 325° until hard, about 1½ hours.

1

2

1 Use all capital letters, glue to a board, and glue on rick rack.

2 Use all capital letters and make dough flowers.

3

4

3 Use all capital letters with 3 dough balloons. The plastic coat hooks are purchased from a hardware store.

4 Use capital and lower case letters for longer words or names. The wreath is made with dough squeezed from a garlic press.

INDEX

About the Author

Paulette Jarvey grew up in Anaheim, California, and moved to Oregon in 1969. She, her husband, Mike, and two sons, Shawn, 12, and Adam, 9, live on two acres in the Canby countryside, near Portland.

She started working with dough art eight years ago when she saw some pieces her younger sister had made in a high school class.

In addition to teaching dough art classes for six years, Paulette sells her dough art creations in more than a dozen stores in Oregon and Washington. She also participates in the more than twenty art and craft shows she organizes for shopping centers.

This is Paulette's first book. Her second, *Let's Dough It Again*, was released in November 1982. Both books are self-published. If additional copies of either book are needed please check your local book or craft store. Or, books may be ordered by writing to Paulette at Hot Off the Press, 7212 S. Seven Oaks, Canby, Oregon 97013.